The Garfield Trivia Book

BY: JIM DAVIS

with Bill Tornquist

BALLANTINE BOOKS • NEW YORK

Copyright © 1986 by United Feature Syndicate, Inc.

All rights reserved under International and Pan-American Copyright
Conventions. Published in the United States by Ballantine Books, a
division of Random House, Inc., New York, and simultaneously in
Canada by Random House of Canada Limited, Toronto.

Library of Congress Catalog Card Number: 86-90724

ISBN 0-345-33771-9

Manufactured in the United States of America

First Edition: October 1986

Designed by Gene Siegel

10   9   8   7   6   5   4   3   2   1

Each page of questions in this book could be considered as two complete trivia games. The questions are in two sets and the answers are found on the following page.

Within each set of questions, every question gets progressively tougher. The first question is worth one point; the second question is worth two points; and so on, until you get to the five-point question, which will require a great memory to answer correctly.

Total the points from each set of questions to see how you did. The following rating system can tell you what kind of Garfield fan you are. Good luck!

JIM DAVIS

0–1   **DUMMY** (Brains-wise, you and Odie should get along well)

2–3   **PRETTY AVERAGE** (You have to read the comic strip regularly to reach this level)

4–5   **KINDA BRIGHT** (You have probably read the books to score this high)

6–7   **INTELLIGENT** (You are a bonafide Garfield authority)

8–9   **HIGHLY INTELLIGENT** (You are obviously a zealous fan with a great memory)

10–11   **BRILLIANT** (It must be lonely at the top)

12–13   **NEAR GENIUS** (Jim Davis himself would have trouble scoring this high)

14–15   **GENIUS** (You cheated!)

1. Who is this?

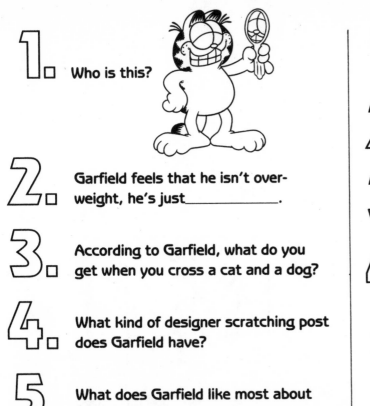

2. Garfield feels that he isn't over-weight, he's just_____.

3. According to Garfield, what do you get when you cross a cat and a dog?

4. What kind of designer scratching post does Garfield have?

5. What does Garfield like most about the inside of cars?

1. What is the full name of Garfield's owner?

2. What is the worst possible day and date for Garfield?

3. When is Garfield's birthday? (Hint: It's in June.)

4. What did Garfield eat when Jon took him to the grocery store?

5. What does Nermal do at night to stay so cute?

1. Garfield.

2. Undertall.

3. A stupid cat.

4. Gucci.

5. The upholstered ceilings.

1. Jon Arbuckle.

2. Monday the 13th.

3. June 19, 1978.

4.

5. He uses curlers and a mudpack.

1. Who is this?

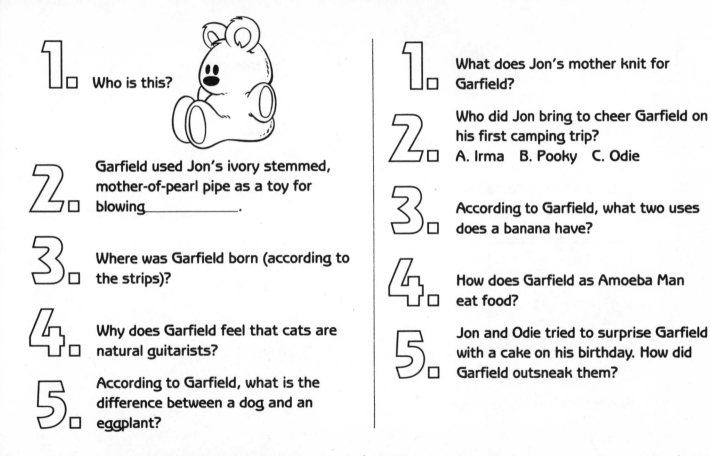

2. Garfield used Jon's ivory stemmed, mother-of-pearl pipe as a toy for blowing_____.

3. Where was Garfield born (according to the strips)?

4. Why does Garfield feel that cats are natural guitarists?

5. According to Garfield, what is the difference between a dog and an eggplant?

1. What does Jon's mother knit for Garfield?

2. Who did Jon bring to cheer Garfield on his first camping trip?
A. Irma   B. Pooky   C. Odie

3. According to Garfield, what two uses does a banana have?

4. How does Garfield as Amoeba Man eat food?

5. Jon and Odie tried to surprise Garfield with a cake on his birthday. How did Garfield outsneak them?

1. Pooky.

2. Bubbles.

3. In the kitchen of Mama Leone's Italian Restaurant.

4.

5. About three I.Q. points.

1. Kitty sweaters.

2. B. Pooky.

3. Food and entertainment (especially when someone slips on the peel).

4. By osmosis.

5. By hiding in the cake.

1. According to Garfield, cats use claws to climb trees, and_____ departments to get down.

2. What does Garfield like best about Tuesday?

3. To feel better about himself when he realized that he was overweight and out of shape, Garfield lowered his _____.

4. How did Garfield try to grow chickens when he visited the farm?

5. Why does Garfield go to sleep at noon on December 24th?

1. Who is this?

2. What is the one thing Garfield loves to hate?

3. The ants ate the apple pie, the wind blew the food, and what else happened to ruin Jon and Garfield's picnic?

4. Who were Billy and Dicky in the Garfield television special, "Garfield In the Rough"?

5. Where did Garfield and Odie hide to keep away from ghosts in the Garfield television special, "The Garfield Halloween Adventure"?

1. Fire.

2. It's not Monday.

3. Expectations.

4. By planting them in the ground.

5.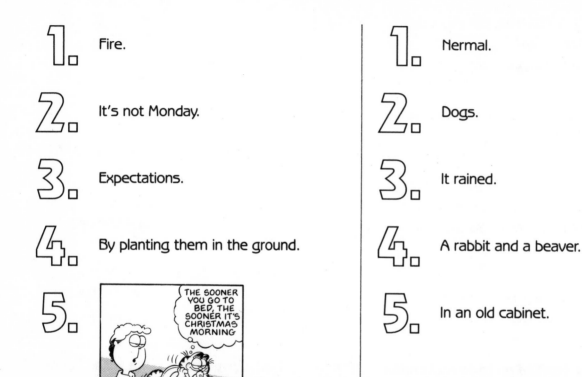

1. Nermal.

2. Dogs.

3. It rained.

4. A rabbit and a beaver.

5. In an old cabinet.

1. Who is this?

2. Garfield says that if Odie's brain were a car, it would be stuck in_____.

3. What kind of food does Garfield hate in his cereal?

4. What was the name of Jon's pet chicken who became noodle soup?

5. What was the name of Garfield's pet ant (who is no longer with us because he was eyeballing Garfield's lasagna)?

1. Why did Liz finally go out with Jon—for his looks or his charm?

2. When Garfield drank too much coffee and overdosed on caffeine, what song did he start to sing? (Hint: "The Chattanooga_____.")

3. What is 6:00 AM Garfield's favorite time for?

4. What is "diet" according to Garfield?

5. What did the scale tell Garfield he was the correct weight for?

1. Jon.

2. Neutral.

3. Raisins.

4. Nadine.

5. Lyle.

1. His charm.

2. Choo Choo.

3. Sleep.

4.

5. An aircraft carrier.

1. ☐ Who is this?

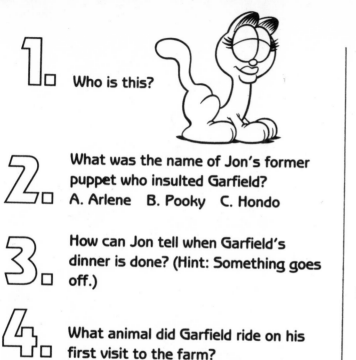

2. ☐ What was the name of Jon's former puppet who insulted Garfield?
A. Arlene   B. Pooky   C. Hondo

3. ☐ How can Jon tell when Garfield's dinner is done? (Hint: Something goes off.)

4. ☐ What animal did Garfield ride on his first visit to the farm?

5. ☐ What did Garfield miss most when Jon took salt out of his diet?

1. ☐ What is Garfield's girlfriend's name?

2. ☐ Who is Nermal?

3. ☐ Where did Garfield hide to ensure that he went with Jon on vacation?

4. ☐ Why didn't Garfield have a good time on his vacation in the tropics?

5. ☐ What is Garfield's only reason for liking Monday mornings?

1. Arlene.

2. C. Hondo

3. The smoke alarm goes off.

4.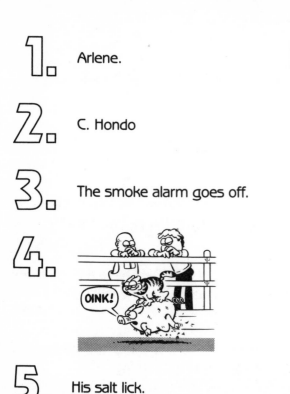

5. His salt lick.

1. Arlene.

2. The world's cutest kitten who comes to visit and bother Garfield.

3. In Jon's suitcase.

4. Because he had such a heavy fur coat on.

5. He doesn't have to go to work.

1. Who is Pooky?

2. When told by Jon that he ate too fast, Garfield reasoned that he was just _____ for the job of eating.

3. Where does Garfield keep his affection?

4. What is the name of the airline Garfield and Jon travel on in the Garfield television special, "Garfield in Paradise"?

5. How many people read the Garfield strip each day?

1. Who is this?

2. The Caped Avenger became the Hankied Avenger when Garfield washed his cape and it_____.

3. What color is Garfield's food bowl?

4. What did Garfield say when Jon told him that they were going to visit the farm? (Hint: He claimed he had to stay home and pluck something.)

5. In how many papers did Garfield first appear?

1. Garfield's teddy bear.

2. Overqualified.

3. In the closet.

4. Inversion Layer Airlines.

5. 100 million.

1. Odie.

2. Shrunk.

3. Green.

4.

5. 40.

1. How does Garfield like his coffee?

2. What is Garfield's lady vet's name?

3. What is Garfield's favorite sport?

4. Who is holding Garfield?

5. In the Garfield television special, "Garfield in Paradise," what was the name of the native who drove the car into the volcano?

1. What did Garfield need to add that was missing from Jon's perfect meal? (Hint: cat_____.)

2. While at the picnic, Garfield agreed with Jon that his cherry pie was the world's best, because 22 million_____ can't all be wrong.

3. Who did Garfield pose as so that he could fly in the airplane cabin with Jon?

4. What is the one thing about the tropics that Garfield loves? (Hint: The tiny_____.)

5. According to Garfield, what do you get when you cross a dieter with a gorilla?

1. Strong enough to sit up and bark.

2. Liz.

3. A brisk nap.

4. Jon's grandmother.

5. Monkey (because he walked like one).

1. Hair.

2.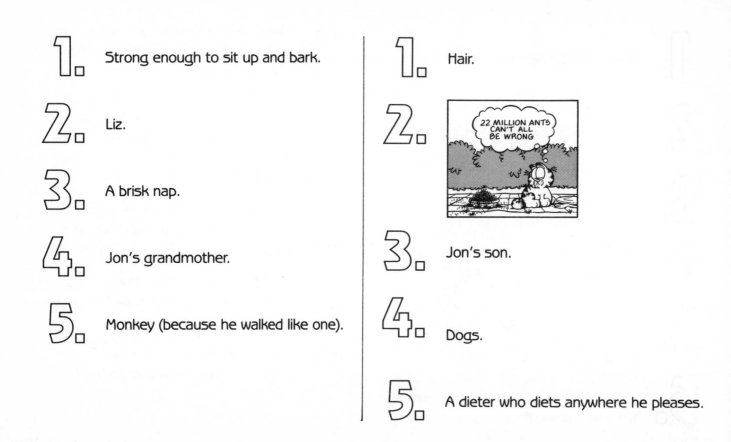

3. Jon's son.

4. Dogs.

5. A dieter who diets anywhere he pleases.

1. What day of the week does Garfield hate?

2. The proper motivation for Garfield to jog is running behind what kind of truck?

3. Who is giving food to Garfield?

HERE, EAT, EAT, EAT

4. According to Garfield, what item in Jon's refrigerator is the only substance harder than a diamond?

5. What hotel chain features Garfield in their advertising?

1. Who is Garfield's confidant?

2. Garfield's reason for not kissing Arlene is "Lips that touch_____ will never touch mine."

3. What was Garfield's excuse for sitting in the freezer to eat his ice cream sundae?

4. Garfield feels he's not intended to marry because he comes from a long line of_____.

5. Where did Jim Davis get the name Garfield?

1. Monday.

2. Ice cream truck.

3. Jon's mother.

4. Jon's leftover pizza.

5. Embassy Suites.

1. Pooky, his teddy bear.

2. Mice.

3.

4. Bachelors.

5. It was his grandfather's middle name.

1. Who does Garfield love most?

2. How many times does Odie turn around before lying down?

3. What color is Garfield's blanket?

4. What did Garfield say when Jon showed him the cows on the farm?

5. What did Amoeba Man, aka Garfield fall in love with?

1. What award has Jim Davis won twice for having the best animated television special?

2. Garfield reasons that if God intended dogs to bark, he would have given them roots and_____.

3. Who is carrying two bales of hay?

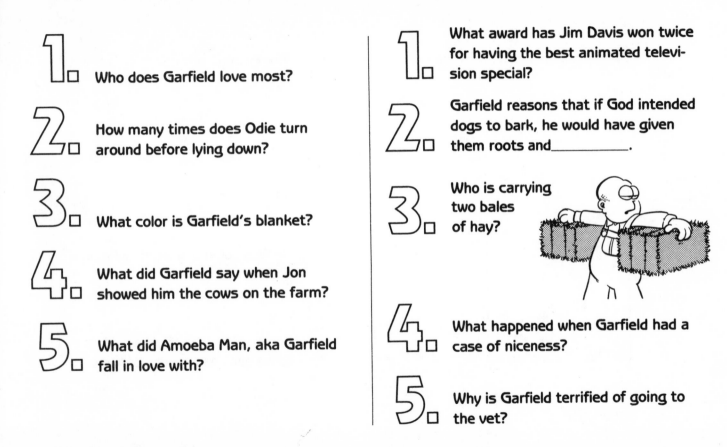

4. What happened when Garfield had a case of niceness?

5. Why is Garfield terrified of going to the vet?

Himself, or course.

 Three times.

 Blue.

 A pillow with a great looking pseudopod.

 The Emmy.

 Leaves.

 Jon's father.

 He was put in a straight jacket in a padded room.

 Because his Uncle Barney did and came back as his Aunt Bernice.

1. In order to get the part in the cat food commercial, Garfield had to be a convincing_____.

2. What was the name of Jon's pet frog?
A. Pooky   B. Lester   C. Herbie

3. Armed against the Sludge Monster, Garfield mangled the liver in the interest of national_____.

4. What is the name of the toy Jon is holding?

GARFIE

5. How did a cat hair get into Madelyn's punch at Jon's New Year's Party?

1. What is the only exercise Garfield enjoys, beside taking a brisk nap?

2. On his first Christmas, Garfield asked Santa for 20 pounds of what?

3. Garfield's philosophy on joggers is "Show me a jogger and I'll show you someone with a thing for_____."

4. In "Garfield in Paradise," what was the name of Jon and Garfield's hotel room?

5. What are the names of Jon's cousin Judy's children?

1. Eater.

2. C. Herbie.

3. Security.

4. Tommy the Clown.

5. Garfield was scuba diving in the punch.

1. Abusing Odie.

2.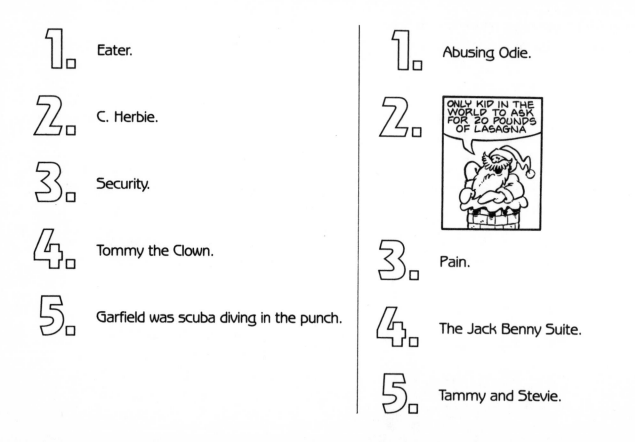

3. Pain.

4. The Jack Benny Suite.

5. Tammy and Stevie.

1. Where did Garfield get stuck for a week when he was trying to surprise the mailman?

2. What is the name of the twelfth Garfield book? (Hint: <u>Garfield Out to</u>_____.)

3. Garfield placed Jon's bunny _____ in a mousetrap instead of a mouse.

4. Who is looking in the mirror?

5. Garfield's Aunt Evelyn is a cat who plucked all her hair so she wouldn't shed. What is she doing now?

1. What was the destination of Garfield and Jon in "Garfield in Paradise"?

2. What is the title of the third Garfield book? (Hint: <u>Garfield Bigger</u> _____ _____.)

3. What does Garfield feel is an emergency measure when he is forced to diet?

4. To attract Liz, Jon wore a manly cologne called "Ode de _____."

5. What is the quote on the bestselling Garfield poster (to date)?

1.

2. Lunch.

3. Slippers.

4. Garfield as Amoeba Man.

5. Posing as a chihuahua.

1. Paradise World.

2. Than Life.

3. Eating mice.

4. Lumberjack.

5. "Have a nice day."

1. Who is the world's cutest kitten?

2. What is the title of the sixth Garfield book? (Hint: <u>Garfield Eats His</u> _____ _____.)

3. What happened at the golf course to make Jon decide never to bring Garfield golfing with him again? (Hint: It happened at the 17th green sandtrap.)

4. What is the name of the frog with Garfield?

5. Why did Garfield not care for Jon's idea of naming all the furnishings and appliances in the house?

1. Where does Garfield do his caterwauling?

2. Jon's mother is always nagging Jon to settle down and marry and what?

3. What does Garfield eat in the credit card commercial?

4. How many times have Jon and Garfield seen "The Sludge Monster Meets Vermin Man"?
A. Nine   B. One   C. Ten

5. How much did Garfield weigh when he was born?

1. Nermal.

2. <u>Heart Out.</u>

3. Garfield used it as a sandbox.

4. Herbie.

5.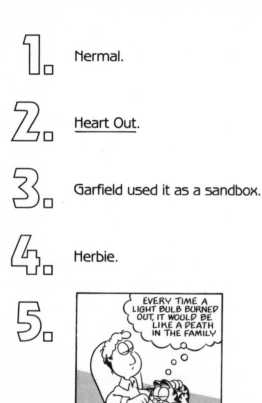

1. On the fence.

2. Eat, eat, eat.

3. A fish.

4. A. Nine.

5. 5 lbs, 6 oz. (The same weight as Jim Davis' son at birth.)

1. What does Garfield have to drink first thing in the morning?

2. What is the title of the fourth Garfield book? (Hint: Garfield_____In.)

3. Who is talking to Jon?

4. What does Garfield always say to Jon?

5. What makes Garfield climb trees?

1. Who did Garfield drop-kick into the next week's strip?

2. What did Doc Boy want to do when he visited Jon and Garfield? (Hint: He wanted to go the airport.)

3. Where does Garfield feel lasagna comes from?

4. What did Garfield accidently spray on himself instead of Jon's deodorant?

5. What was Garfield's grandpa famous for in his day?

1. Coffee.

2. Weighs.

3. Jon's brother, Doc Boy.

4. Nothing. Garfield only thinks; he never speaks.

5.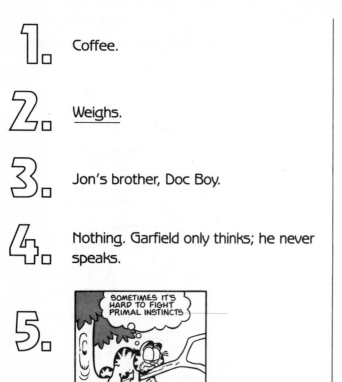

1. Odie.

2. To watch the planes land.

3. Heaven, of course.

4. Spray starch.

5. He was the best ratter in Middletown.

1. What jar does Garfield like to hide in?

2. Where in the kitchen does Garfield hide the raisins from his raisin toast?

3. So Garfield would play with Odie, what did Jon spray Odie with?

4. Who is Jon talking with?

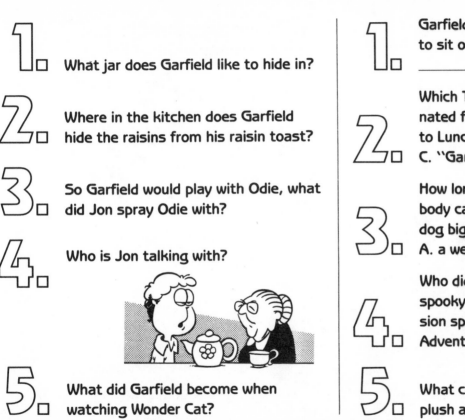

5. What did Garfield become when watching Wonder Cat?

1. Garfield's favorite place in the house to sit on chilly mornings is over the _____ vent.

2. Which TV show had an album nominated for a Grammy? A. "Garfield Out to Lunch" B. Here Comes Garfield" C. "Garfield in the Rough"

3. How long was Garfield to be in the body cast after he tangled with a dog bigger than himself? A. a week B. a day C. a month

4. Who did Garfield and Odie meet in the spooky house in the Garfield television special, "The Garfield Halloween Adventure"?

5. What company makes the Garfield plush animals?

1. The cookie jar.

2. In a drawer.

3. Essence of Lasagna.

4. His Aunt Gussie.

5. A Wonder Cat Cadet.

1.

2. B. "Here Comes Garfield."

3. A. a week.

4. The Old Man.

5. R. Dakin & Company.

1. When he and Jon visited the Hamiltons, where did Garfield learn he should never sharpen his claws? (Hint: in the bedroom.)

2. On what cartoon strip did Jim Davis first apprentice? A. Peanuts B. Garfield C. Tumbleweeds.

3. How did Garfield react when Pooky's arm fell off?

4. What did the baby chick mistake Garfield for?

5. How far ahead does Jim Davis work on the Garfield strip?

1. According to Garfield, life is like a poker game, because if you don't win, you _____.

2. According to Garfield cats are little people with_____and fangs.

3. Garfield says eating is social, but when you diet, you diet _____.

4. Who is Garfield holding?

5. What was the first national TV interview show Jim Davis appeared on?

1.

2. C. Tumbleweeds.

3. He fainted.

4. His daddy.

5. 8 weeks for daily strips; 12 weeks for Sunday strips.

1. Lose.

2. Fur.

3. Alone.

4. Stretch, his rubber chicken.

5. "The Today Show."

1. What is Garfield's favorite food?

2. What cat disease was Garfield suffering from when he went everywhere wearing a flowered shirt?

3. Who is Garfield pretending to be?

4. What advice does Garfield give to those who complain they have cat hairs all over the house when company visits?

5. What was the name of Garfield and Odie's rowboat in "The Garfield Halloween Adventure"?

1. What is the name of Jon's other pet?

2. When eating milk and cookies, what does Garfield always run out of first?

3. Garfield feels dogs should be banned from this country because they are _____our nation's fire hydrants.

4. Who sings all the theme songs for the Garfield television specials?

5. In how many languages does the Garfield strip appear?

1. Lasagna!

2.

GARFIELD, YOU HAVE THE HAWAIIAN CAT FLU. YOU'RE GOING TO HAVE TO LIE AROUND ALL WEEK

OH, DARN

JIM DAVIS

3. The Caped Avenger.

4. Never have anyone over to your house.

5. Carolyn (after Jim Davis' wife).

1. Odie.

2. Milk.

3. Rusting.

4. Lou Rawls.

5. Twelve.

1. According to Garfield, what is the one word you should never say to an animal person? (Hint: It rhymes with "mixed".)

2. A Garfield quote: "As you walk down the path of life, stop and _____ the flowers along the way."

3. What did Garfield name this mouse?

WHAT'S YOUR NAME, MOUSE?

OH, GEE. I DON'T THINK I HAVE A NAME

JIM DAVIS

4. What does Garfield consider suicide, exercise, and dieting to be?

5. Where did Garfield go to try surfing?

1. What warm piece of furniture does Garfield like to sleep on?

2. What was wrong with the motel pool in the Garfield television special, "Garfield in Paradise?"

3. Rather than getting into his own bed with his muddy feet, where did Garfield go?

4. Because he loves happy endings, what is Garfield's favorite movie?

5. Who does the voice of Garfield on his television specials?

1. Fixed.

2.

3. Squeak.

4. Three forms of self-abuse.

5. The local birdbath.

1. The television set.

2. It was empty.

3. Jon's bed.

4. "Old Yeller."

5. Lorenzo Music.

1. In the Macy's Day Parade in 1984, Garfield made his first appearance as a_____.

2. What insect is Garfield afraid of?

3. Who were Garfield's two prime suspects in the Pooky kidnapping?

4. When is Garfield's 10th birthday?

5. What year did the first Garfield TV show air?

1. The book Garfield In Disguise was based on which Garfield television special?

2. What animal did Jim Davis try to create a strip around before Garfield?

3. Who is talking to Jon and Garfield?

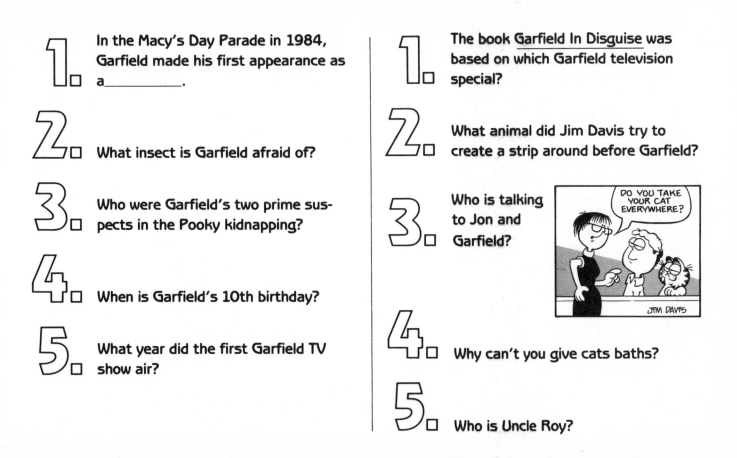

DO YOU TAKE YOUR CAT EVERYWHERE?

JIM DAVIS

4. Why can't you give cats baths?

5. Who is Uncle Roy?

 Balloon.

2. Spiders.

3. Jon and Odie.

4. June 19, 1988.

5. 1982.

 "The Garfield Halloween Adventure."

2. A gnat.

3. Irma, the waitress.

4.

5. A television host Garfield watches.

1. What kind of attacks does Garfield have?

2. Who did Jon take out on a date?

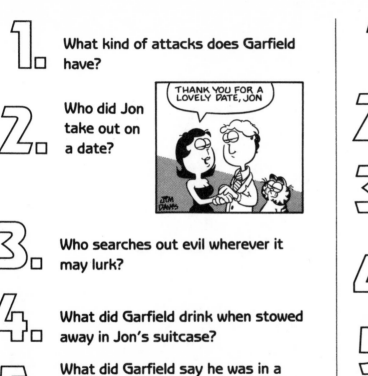

THANK YOU FOR A LOVELY DATE, JON

JIM DAVIS

3. Who searches out evil wherever it may lurk?

4. What did Garfield drink when stowed away in Jon's suitcase?

5. What did Garfield say he was in a former life when Jon asked him why he ate so much?

1. If reincarnation existed, Garfield would come back as a _____ catcher.

2. Where do Jon's parents live?

3. What is the name of the syndicate that distributes Garfield?

4. Garfield left the faucet running when they went on vacation so that what collection of his wouldn't dry out?

5. What did Garfield have for lunch when he and Jon visited the zoo?

1. Nap attacks!

2. Liz, Garfield's vet.

3. The Caped Avenger.

4. Jon's aftershave lotion.

5.

1. Dog.

2. On a farm.

3. United Feature Syndicate, Inc.

4. His sponge collection.

5. A rare $300.00 parrot.

1. Jim Davis and Garfield appear in a television commercial for what credit card company?

2. Garfield, Odie, and Jon go camping in which television special?

3. Does Jim Davis own any cats?

4. Who is walking with Garfield?

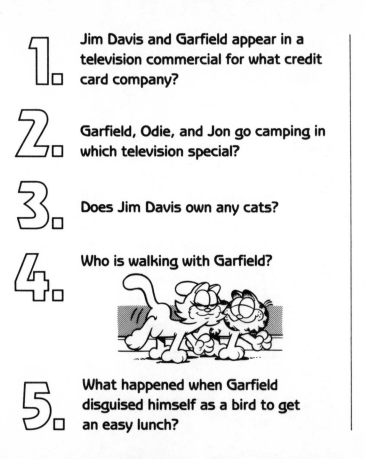

5. What happened when Garfield disguised himself as a bird to get an easy lunch?

1. Garfield was classified in the _____ division of the cat show.

2. What is the name of the first Garfield television special? (Hint: "Here _____ _____.")

3. What day of the week is Lasagna Day?

4. What was Garfield's food-oriented suggestion for naming Jon's goldfish?

5. Why does Garfield hate his designer sweater?

1. American Express.

2. "Garfield in the Rough."

3. No (his wife is allergic). However, he grew up with 25.

4. His mother.

5. He was chased by a bunch of cats.

1. Fat.

2. "_____ Comes Garfield."

3. Everyday!

4.

5. Because the lizard keeps eating out the armpit.

1. According to Jon, Garfield's glandular problem is an_____mouth gland.

2. Garfield's version of a Will Rogers quote is "I never met a _____ I didn't like."

3. What is the name of Garfield's rubber chicken?

4. Why does Garfield hate cold floors in the morning, even more than the average person?

5. Who are these two people?

1. Garfield won't eat table scraps because he considers that to be what kind of food?

2. What did Jon, Liz, and Garfield do on their first date?

3. Who saved Garfield from drowning in the river in the Garfield television special, "The Garfield Halloween Adventure"?

4. What did Jon stick in his ear to help Garfield and himself get out of the depression they were in?

5. Who does Nermal belong to?

1. Overactive.

2.

3. Stretch.

4. Because he has twice as many feet to put on them.

5. Jon's neighbors, Hubert and Reba.

1. Dog food.

2. They saw a movie.

3. Odie.

4. A banana.

5. Jon's parents.

1. Jon bought Garfield another rubber mouse, because Garfield said the other one was eaten by a _____cat.

2. What did Jon tell Garfield was under the bed to get him to clean under it?

3. Who is the Caped Avenger's (aka Garfield) source of security?

4. What was Garfield's excuse for eating Jon's goldfish?

5. Who is Garfield with in this picture?

1. What does Garfield like to do to Jon's furniture?

2. According to Garfield eating tips, when is the only time you should snack?

3. What does Garfield feel is worse than Odie's bark?

4. What was the first thing Garfield did when he was out of the body cast?

5. Who was supposed to take care of Garfield while Jon was away on vacation?

1. Rubber.

2. Lasagna.

3. Pooky, the bear.

4. An ethnic weakness.

5. His grandpa.

1.

2. Between meals.

3. His breath.

4. He smacked Odie with it.

5. Jon's Aunt Gussie.

1. According to Garfield, life is like a hot bath because the longer you stay in, the more_____you get.

2. In what food did Jon put Garfield's vitamins so that he would eat them?

3. Why was Garfield disappointed when he tasted the dogie biscuit?

4. Who did Garfield go trick or treating as in the Garfield television special, "The Garfield Halloween Adventure"?

5. Who is on the fence with Garfield?

1. What kind of plant of Jon's does Garfield always eat?

2. What mouse got sucked up in Jon's vacuum cleaner?

3. Which Garfield television special won an Emmy for the best animated feature in 1985?

4. What is the name of Jim Davis' company?

5. What was the name of Chief Rama Lama's tribe in the Garfield television special, "Garfield in Paradise"?

1. Wrinkled.

2. Lasagna.

3.

4. Orange Beard, the Pirate.

5. Odie, as Mr. Skins.

1. His fern.

2. Squeak.

3. "Garfield in the Rough."

4. PAWS, Inc.

5. The Ding Dongs.

1. What does Garfield like to chase in the streets?

2. Who was Garfield's first mate in "The Garfield Halloween Adventure"?

3. According to Garfield, what is warm, fun to lie in, must be chased, but can never be caught?

4. Where did Garfield discover Pooky?

5. Who is in the tree with Garfield?

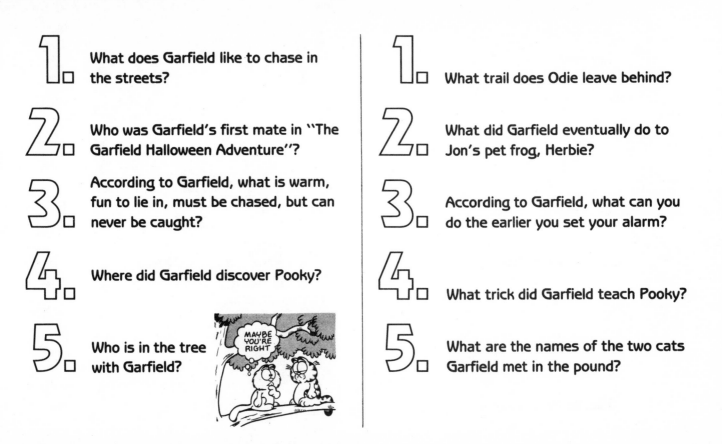

1. What trail does Odie leave behind?

2. What did Garfield eventually do to Jon's pet frog, Herbie?

3. According to Garfield, what can you do the earlier you set your alarm?

4. What trick did Garfield teach Pooky?

5. What are the names of the two cats Garfield met in the pound?

1. Cars.

2. Odie.

3. Sunlight.

4. In a dresser drawer.

5. Ed.

1. Slobber.

2. He ate him.

3.

4. To play dead.

5. Guido and Fluffy.

1. What color is Garfield's nose?

2. According to Garfield, television commercials are too long to sit through and too short for what?

3. What does Jon do for a living?

4. In Garfield's dream of large breakfasts, he ate a giant pancake. What did he actually eat in his sleep?

5. Who is talking to Jon?

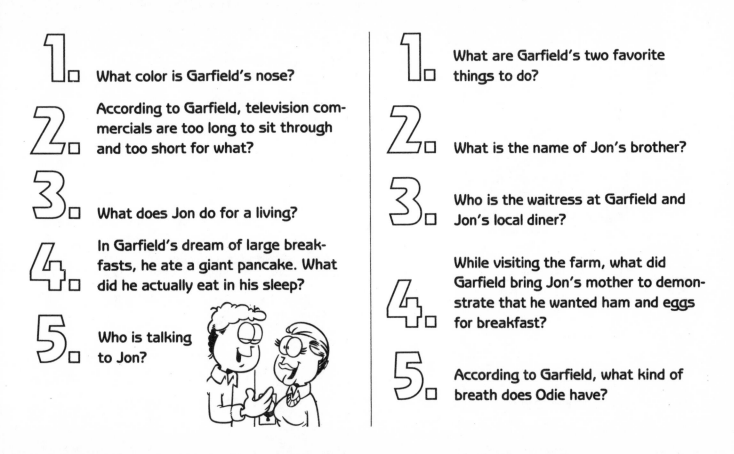

1. What are Garfield's two favorite things to do?

2. What is the name of Jon's brother?

3. Who is the waitress at Garfield and Jon's local diner?

4. While visiting the farm, what did Garfield bring Jon's mother to demonstrate that he wanted ham and eggs for breakfast?

5. According to Garfield, what kind of breath does Odie have?

1. What character, who comes to the house once a day, does Garfield like to abuse?

2. Who is Garfield pretending to be?

AHEE AH-EE AH!

3. What is the name of the first Garfield book?

4. Why doesn't Jon want Garfield to eat chicken anymore?

5. What use does Garfield make of Jon's toothbrush?

1. What always happens when Garfield sings on the fence?

2. What does Jon use as an alarm clock in the morning?

3. What physical characteristic does Arlene have that Garfield makes fun of?

4. How did Garfield get to eat 12 boxes of Girl Scout cookies?

5. Why does Garfield attack the mailman?

1. The mailman.

2. Tarzan.

3. Garfield at Large.

4. He doesn't want him to choke on the bones.

5. He uses it as a backscratcher.

1. Things are thrown at him.

2. Garfield, when he's ready for breakfast.

3.

4. He mugged a Girl Scout.

5. He doesn't think dogs should have all the fun.

1. What is the only thing that gets Garfield out of bed in the morning?

2. What does Jon claim Garfield's passion for food is only exceeded by?

3. What color is Nermal?

4. What does Arlene consider Garfield's most outstanding feature to be?

5. Who are these two characters with Garfield?

1. Complete Garfield's expression: "Big, fat, _____ _____."

2. What did Garfield give Odie as thanks for saving his life in the Garfield television special, "The Garfield Halloween Adventure"?

3. What animal escaped from the zoo and was on the loose in the Garfield television special, "Garfield in the Rough"?

4. While visiting the farm, what did Garfield fall into and get muddy?

5. Why does Garfield feel that kittens are like strings?

1. Hunger.

2.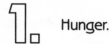

3. Gray.

4. He's fat.

5. Guido and Fluffy.

1. Hairy Deal.

2. Garfield gave back Odie's trick-or-treat candy.

3. A panther.

4. Hog waller.

5. Every yo-yo wants one.

1. Who is Garfield chasing?

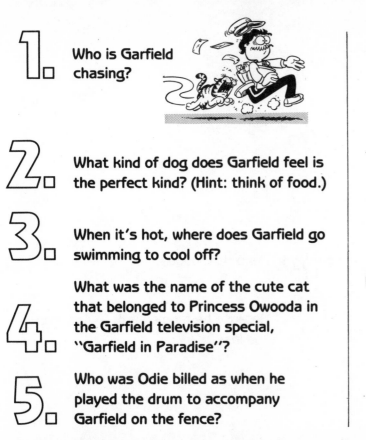

2. What kind of dog does Garfield feel is the perfect kind? (Hint: think of food.)

3. When it's hot, where does Garfield go swimming to cool off?

4. What was the name of the cute cat that belonged to Princess Owooda in the Garfield television special, "Garfield in Paradise"?

5. Who was Odie billed as when he played the drum to accompany Garfield on the fence?

1. Garfield is fat and _____ and proud of it.

2. What is the title of the tenth Garfield book? (Hint: Garfield Makes It _____.)

3. What is the name of Garfield's cat friend who has lived his whole life in a tree with squirrels?

4. Who does Jon fall in love with in the Garfield television special, "Garfield in Paradise"?

5. Why did Garfield have to be in a body cast?

1. The mailman.

2. A hot dog.

3.

4. Mai Tai.

5. Mr. Skins.

1. Lazy.

2. Big.

3. Ed.

4. Princess Owooda.

5. Because he tangled with a giant dog and lost.

1. How many toes does Garfield have?

2. When it comes to eating, Garfield claims he's a:
A. novice   B. slob   C. genius

3. According to Garfield's history of cats, who is this?

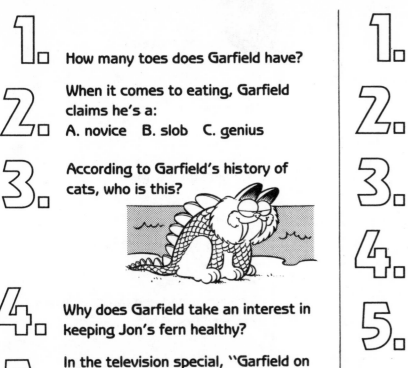

4. Why does Garfield take an interest in keeping Jon's fern healthy?

5. In the television special, "Garfield on the Town," why was Fluffy in the pound?

1. Who does Garfield protect from Jon?

2. What holiday is the fourth Garfield television special about?

3. What is the title of the second Garfield television special?

4. Why did Garfield think the baby in the carriage looked so beautiful?

5. What happened when Jon invited some girls to go double-dating with his brother, Doc Boy?

Fourteen.

3. The very first cat to crawl out of the sea.

4. To fatten it up for slaughter.

5. He couldn't be housebroken.

1. Squeak, the mouse

2. Halloween.

3. "Garfield on the Town."

4. Because it looked like him.

5. They screamed and ran away when they saw Doc Boy.

1. What does Odie always have hanging out?

2. Jon actually kidnapped Pooky to sew his _____ back on.

3. Who is the mean neighbor who gets Garfield and Odie into trouble in the television special, ''Here Comes Garfield''?

4. What household object is one of Garfield's best friends?

5. Who is Jon holding?

1. How many whiskers does Garfield have?

2. What is the title of the fifth Garfield book? (Hint: <u>Garfield Takes</u> _____ _____.)

3. What happens when Garfield plays with the window shades?

4. Why won't Nermal ever grow to be full-sized cat?

5. What is the name of Hubert and Reba's pet?

1. His tongue.

2. Arm.

3. Hubert.

4. The mirror.

5. Hondo, the puppet.

1. Six.

2. <u>the Cake.</u>

3.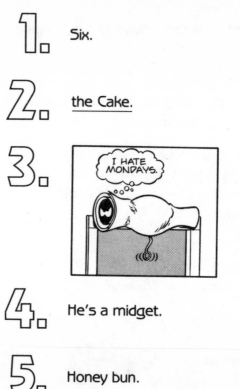

4. He's a midget.

5. Honey bun.